W9-BLJ-201

SERVING AS A CHURCH USHER

FORMERLY TITLED *THE USHER'S MANUAL*

PAUL E. ENGLE, SERIES EDITOR
LESLIE PARROTT

ZONDERVAN™

GRAND RAPIDS, MICHIGAN 49530 USA

ZONDERVAN™

Serving as a Church Usher
Copyright © 1970 by Zondervan
Copyright © 2002 by Leslie Parrott

Formerly titled *The Usher's Manual*

Requests for information should be addressed to:

Zondervan, *Grand Rapids, Michigan 49530*

Library of Congress Cataloging-in-Publication Data

Parrott, Leslie, 1922–
　　[Usher's manual]
　　Serving as a church usher / Leslie Parrott.
　　　　p.　　cm. — (Zondervan practical ministry guides)
　　Originally published: The usher's manual. Grand Rapids :
Zondervan, 1970.
　　ISBN 0-310-24763-2
　　1. Church ushers.　I. Title.　II. Series.
BV705 .P33　2002
254 — dc21

2002008299

Interior design by Sherri L. Hoffman

Printed in the United States of America

04 05 06 07 08 /❖ DC/ 10 9 8 7 6 5

CONTENTS

PREFACE

Ushering has been a stepchild in many churches for too long. The usher is a personal representative of Jesus Christ who meets people on a person-to-person basis when they first arrive at church. As such, the usher's ministry of service must be recognized as a profoundly important one.

In many small churches, these stepchildren called "ushers" are kept from sight most of the time, at least until collection time, and then they fade from sight again. Morale among ushers is low, and there is little feeling of being needed or of belonging.

In other churches the enthusiasm of the ushers and greeters is contagious. Their skills have been developed and their attitudes are good because they have accepted the challenge for a high standard of excellence they know the pastor and people have come to expect. In these churches the ushers are included in planning and communications on an equal level with choir members and Sunday school teachers. The head usher is chosen with the same care traditionally used in selecting Sunday school superintendents and youth leaders. The silent ministry of these efficient, people-oriented ushers is a blessing to every church service.

Every church can have an effective group of ushers. *Serving as a Church Usher* is intended as a guide to reaching this goal. Begin by reading the guidelines in "How to Use This Guide." Then continue the study of the chapters as a reference book and training tool for developing the ministry of ushering in the church.

Although both males and females serve as ushers in many of today's churches, in most cases I've elected to use masculine pronouns when referring to them to facilitate ease of reading.

Many ideas in *Serving as a Church Usher* have come from my observance of the outstanding ministry performed by the boards of ushers in churches I've served as pastor. I am grateful for their faithful service and dedication.

—Leslie Parrott

HOW TO USE THIS GUIDE

Serving as a Church Usher is intended to fill three needs in the church. First, it is hoped that pastors, ushers, and congregations will see the high importance of ushering and be motivated to lift the standard of excellence among ushers to the level of a "ministry" in local churches.

Second, the questions raised in this guide are intended to make it more useful as a reference tool. No two ushering situations are alike. Solutions to ushering problems offered in this book may be inapplicable in some situations. *Serving as a Church Usher* is not intended as an arbitrary authority but as a point of reference. All solutions to specific ushering problems must be worked out on a basis of common sense in the local situation. Taken as a guide, this book can be a useful tool for reference in these matters.

Third, *Serving as a Church Usher* is intended to be a training tool for pastors and head ushers to use in local churches. Every person on the board of ushers in a local church should own a copy. It should be read, studied in ushers' meetings, and used for training drills. Questions for discussion and training exercises are included at the end of each chapter.

The five chapters may be used for five training sessions as follows:

Chapter 1 ("The Ministry of Ushering") is intended to inspire and motivate ushers in making their work a ministry—not a job—in the church. The pastor is usually the best person to present this material and to inspire the ushers to a new level of usefulness. "An Usher's Prayer" at the close of the chapter may be read in unison by participants at the close of the session. "An Usher's Commission" may be used by the pastor in a public installation service for ushers.

Chapter 2 ("The Functions of an Usher") deals with the attitudes of an usher toward people, toward the service in progress, and toward himself. These attitudes are more important than many suspect in determining the final quality of service rendered by an usher. The second half of the chapter deals with the techniques of ushering as they relate to the people and to the church service. Use of this chapter should involve (1) a consultation with the pastor, (2) a study of the church bulletin and usual format of the services, and (3) times of practicing in the sanctuary.

Chapter 3 ("An Usher's Standard of Excellence") may be used in a discussion session. Assign several ushers to present the main points in the section titled "A More Excellent Way" (pages 44–46). Follow their remarks with a discussion period. Use the same technique with the section titled "Exhibiting the Fruit of the Spirit" (pages 46–48). These presentations and discussions will be useful and productive to the degree they are directly related to the specific attitudes, techniques, and problems of ushers in your church.

Chapter 4 ("The Authority and Responsibility of Ushers") is critical in the administration of an ushering ministry. A panel presentation may be made by (1) the pastor, (2) the lay leader of the church board, and (3) the head usher. This session would be a good time to bring in the Sunday school superintendent, the choir director, and the musicians. If there is a separate greeters committee in the church alongside the ushers, the chairman of this group should be invited as well. To clarify the issues in this chapter, questions can be directed to the panel by the others in attendance.

Chapter 5 ("Ushers as Greeters") may be used in a training session. Suggestions are made at the end of the chapter on how to train people in the techniques of remembering names and introducing people.

ONE

The Ministry of Ushering

PREACHING, TEACHING, MUSIC, AND USHERING

Any act of Christian service that helps direct people into fellowship with Jesus Christ is a ministry. The most prominent ministry in the church is *preaching*. Paul wrote to the Romans, "How can they believe in the one of whom they have not heard? And how can they hear without someone preaching to them?" (Romans 10:14).

The second prominent ministry in the church is *teaching*. Next to the preaching of the gospel, Martin Luther believed that teaching was the highest calling of humankind. Teaching is mentioned many times in the New Testament and is included among the spiritual gifts. The pastor who preaches without teaching, or the church that evangelizes without instructing, is not only obscuring the cross of Christ but failing to provide the Holy Spirit with opportunity to carry out one of his most important functions. Jesus told his disciples, "The Counselor, the Holy Spirit, whom the Father will send in my name, will teach you all things and will remind you of everything I have said to you" (John 14:26). Later he added, "When he, the Spirit of truth, comes, he will guide you into all truth" (16:13). Paul wrote to Timothy, "The Lord's servant must not quarrel; instead, he must be kind to everyone, able to teach, not resentful. Those who oppose him he must gently instruct" (2 Timothy 2:24–25).

The third great ministry in the church is *music*. According to Paul, music is at least on a par with teaching as a ministry in the church: "Let the word of Christ dwell in you richly as you teach and admonish one another with all wisdom, and as you sing psalms, hymns and spiritual songs" (Colossians 3:16).

The fourth great ministry of the church is *ushering*. Paul, who believed in the power of preaching, the importance of teaching, and the ministry of music, also wrote, "Everything should be done in a fitting and orderly way" (1 Corinthians 14:40). Ushers are given the responsibility of tending to the details of each service so that it is conducted in an orderly fashion.

The importance of the ushers' ministry caused one pastor to say, "If I had to choose between losing the ushers or the choir, I would rather lose the choir." This undoubtedly was an exaggeration intended to emphasize the importance of the ushering ministry in his church. But it is a fact that it will take music from a very extraordinary choir to overcome the poor work of inefficient ushers. Though of unequal importance, preaching, teaching, singing, and ushering are so closely related to one another that one does not tend to rise above the other in a given church. The preachers, teachers, musicians, and ushers all need each other!

USHERS IN THE OLD TESTAMENT

Ushers in the Old Testament tabernacle—and later in the temple—were called doorkeepers. The psalmist, writing for the director of music in the temple, understood the importance of ushers when he said, "How lovely is your dwelling place, O LORD Almighty! . . . Blessed are those who dwell in your house; they are ever praising you. . . . Better is one day in your courts than a thousand elsewhere; I would rather be a doorkeeper in the house of my God than dwell in the tents of the wicked" (Psalm 84:1, 4, 10). One of the functions of doorkeepers in the Old Testament was to receive the collections from the people. We read in 2 Kings 22:4, "Go up to Hilkiah the high priest and have him get ready the money that has been brought into the temple of the LORD, which the doorkeepers have collected from the people." The Old Testament chronicler spoke of Shallum and his "fellow gatekeepers," who were "responsible for guarding the entrance to the dwelling of the LORD" (1 Chronicles 9:19). The preacher in Ecclesiastes wrote about the day "when the keepers of the house tremble" (Ecclesiastes 12:3). And in Ezekiel's vision of a future temple, he saw space reserved for the priests, the musicians, and two sets of ushers— "the priests who have charge of the temple" and "the priests who have charge of the altar" (Ezekiel 40:45–46).

USHERS IN THE NEW TESTAMENT

In the New Testament the temple ushers were given unusual authority, evidently as uniformed guards. In the book of Acts, "the captain of the temple" and "the officers" are referred to several times in connection with arrests and general handling of the crowds. It was these doorkeepers, or ushers, who carried out the high priest's orders in the persecutions against the apostles immediately following Pentecost and thirty years later in the arrest and maltreatment of Paul.

Jesus used his disciples as ushers on many occasions. They prepared the way for his coming, they introduced people to him, and they directed the people who had come to hear him speak or to be touched by his healing hands. On one occasion Jesus gave a sharp warning to the disciples, who as ushers had endeavored to keep children away from him. On still another occasion Jesus directed the disciples in organizing a congregation of five thousand men plus women and children to be seated in groups of fifty. Then, with Jesus supplying the unending loaves and fish, the disciples served the hungry multitude.

The first church board also served as ushers: "So the Twelve gathered all the disciples together and said, 'It would not be right for us to neglect the ministry of the word of God in order to wait on tables. Brothers, choose seven men from among you who are known to be full of the Spirit and wisdom. We will turn this responsibility over to them and will give our attention to prayer and the ministry of the word.' This proposal pleased the whole group" (Acts 6:2–5). The character of these first deacons is spelled out clearly.

WHAT MAKES A GOOD USHER?

The three qualities of Christlike people expounded by Jesus in the Sermon on the Mount are exemplified in the ministry of church ushers. First, the ministry of ushering is like salt that makes everything more palatable and serves as a general preservative against deterioration. Jesus did not say, "You ought to be the salt of the earth"; he said, "You are the salt of the earth" (Matthew 5:13, emphasis added). And Paul said, "Let your conversation be always full of grace, seasoned with salt" (Colossians 4:6). A good usher adds a tang of joy rather than a tinge of drabness to a churchgoer's Sunday worship experience. Also, the ministry of an usher is like salt because salt can never do its work until it is brought into close contact with the substance on which it is to make its influence. The church ushers, pastors, musicians, and teachers come into direct contact with more people in a given service than anyone else who ministers to them. The ministry of salt is silent, inconspicuous, and sometimes completely unnoticed. But it is there—in a powerful and useful way.

Also, a good usher, like "a city on a hill" (Matthew 5:14), becomes a landmark to churchgoers who learn to depend on him. Stability helps overcome other weaknesses an usher may have. The first glimpse of an usher on whom a churchgoer has come to depend brings an internal sense of welcome repose. The churchgoer thinks, "Someone is on hand who is interested in me!" It's not uncommon for an usher to become an adviser, a source of information, or, better yet, an intermediary between the needs of a specific person and the resources available through the pastor, musicians, and teachers of the church.

Third, a good usher is like a lamp. Jesus said, "Neither do people light a lamp and put it under a bowl. Instead they put it on its stand, and it gives light to everyone in the house" (Matthew 5:15). A lamp brings warmth and welcome to all who are in the room. One shining candle can brighten the conversation in a room and bring an inner feeling of warmth and joy. Just as a lamp dispels the darkness and brings emotional warmth to a room, so the ministry of an usher can make a similar intangible contribution to all who experience the light he allows to shine through himself.

Jesus concluded his discussion on godly character by saying, "Let your light shine before men, that they may see your good deeds and praise your Father in heaven" (Matthew 5:16).

The nature of Christian character is to radiate; it cannot help but shine. The radiance of this glory is not for "self" but for the kingdom of God. The ministry of an usher is not intended to bring glory to himself but to God. Just as a pastor preaches in the Spirit and a musician sings in the Spirit, the usher must do his work in the power of the Holy Spirit, bringing glory to God in the Lord's house on the Lord's Day.

WHY USHERS ARE SO IMPORTANT

One day in Chicago William Wrigley Jr. looked mournfully down at the streams of customers who stood before the ticket boxes at Wrigley Field to get refunds for the baseball seats they had bought but could not locate. While Mr. Wrigley groaned inwardly about the loss of his customers, Andy Frain, a young man in his early twenties, approached the financial wizard and begged for the job of head usher at the great baseball stadium. Desperate for a solution to his seating problems, Wrigley hired him.

In only a few years Andy Frain completely revolutionized ushering at Wrigley Field and made himself "king of the ushers." Even more important, he made ushering a respectable new vocation. Frain organized a school for his men, whom he had handpicked from many applicants. He gave them blackboard drills and showed them training films. At the completion of the training, each recruit had to pass a test before doing a two-week internship of field work and then receiving a diploma and a blue uniform with brass buttons and gold stripes.

In a few years Andy Frain expanded his ushering reach to include many of the great auditoriums and arenas in the United States. During a single year his ushers handled a number of people equal to the entire population of the United States. Through his branch offices in every major American city, Frain supervised every large gathering in the nation. Even the Democrats and Republicans agreed on something: Andy Frain's ushers would handle the crowds at both national conventions.

While the need for good ushers has been recognized and met in the large secular arenas, the need is also being recognized by churches, both large and small. Clergy are relying more and more on efficient ushers to handle problems that relate to the congregation. There are three reasons why the importance of the ministry of ushering is becoming more recognized.

First, an usher is a forerunner, often the first official representative of Jesus Christ seen by people who enter God's house. As John the Baptist was a forerunner for the ministry of Jesus Christ, the church usher is a forerunner for all the other ministries in the congregation. Teachers meet students in the classroom. Pastors face the people from behind a pulpit after worshipers are assembled in their places. Choir members sing with their eyes fastened on the director, not on the people. But before members of the congregation ever see the teachers, pastor, or musicians, they come face-to-face with a church usher. As an official representative of the church and of Jesus Christ, the usher has an enormous obligation to help lead people into readiness for learning, worshiping, and evangelism. The attitude the usher demonstrates in the foyer of the church is a forerunner of the ministry to be experienced in the sanctuary and sets the spiritual tone for everything else to come. An usher in the lobby can enhance or detract from the ministry in the worship center by the way he administers his duties.

Second, the church usher may be the only individual contact the church makes directly with persons during their attendance in a service. Preachers, teachers, and musicians minister to people in groups, while ushers minister to individuals. A Spirit-directed word of encouragement, reassurance, or kindness may be the most significant ministry some people receive in their church attendance experience. Only a few can linger to meet the pastor, to ask questions of the teachers, and to talk with the musicians, but everyone may have a firsthand encounter with the ministry of a good usher.

Third, the usher is the only person whose functions cannot be replaced or omitted. Sometimes preaching is omitted, and it is not unusual to have a service without a choir. And on occasion classes get dismissed. But there is no substitute for the work of ushers in any church service regardless of its character. At weddings, funerals, communion services, evangelistic campaigns, patriotic rallies, cantatas, Christmas plays, films, and any other kind of church meeting, ushers are vitally important.

AN USHER'S PRAYER

May I, dear Lord, in church today, fulfill my assignment in a Christlike way. Make me efficient in what I do, effective in what I say, understanding by the way I feel about people, and helpful in the attitudes I have toward them. Make me a coworker with the pastor, the church musicians, the teachers—and most of all, Lord, with you. Save me from hurtful words and harmful deeds. Make people glad they came to our church today because the Holy Spirit ministered to their needs through the sermons and prayers of the pastor, through the music of the organist and singers, through the explanations of knowledge-able teachers, and through the ministry of ushers like me. In Jesus' name. Amen.

AN USHER'S COMMISSION

At the beginning of another year the church gives you this fresh commission, new and yet old. Allow the hospitality of this church to become incarnate in you. Wrap every word and clothe every action in the spirit of human kindness. May your kind of Christianity help people let down their guards, open their hearts, and relax their minds for the worship of God and direction of his Holy Spirit. Be understanding with the difficult person. Exercise compassion with all kinds of people. Learn to be efficient but not at the expense of kindness. And accept from the pastor and congregation this assignment that ranks in importance with the other ministries of this church. May your highest good be the kindness of human understanding, your greatest virtue the stability of a person in Christ, and your most effective tool the indwelling presence of the Holy Spirit of Christ.

QUESTIONS FOR REFLECTION AND DISCUSSION

1. The purpose of this chapter is to help ushers see the prime impor-
    tance of their assignment as a ministry for Jesus Christ and his
    church. What can you do to champion this passion for ministry?

2. Read Matthew 9:2–8 alone or together as a group of ushers. What
    does this account of four "ushers" bringing a paralytic to Jesus
    teach you about the ministry of ushering?

3. In what way is the work of an usher like salt?

4. In what ways can the presence of a good usher be like a lamp that
    gives emotional warmth to a church?

5. What church ushers have you known who became real person-to-
    person ministers as ushers? Tell about them.

6. This chapter (and each succeeding chapter in this guide) may be
    presented in a training session by the pastor or another qualified
    person well respected by the participants. (The speaker should be
    a person who is able to motivate others.)

    If you decide to hold a training session for ushers in your
    church, assign certain people to read the following Old Testament
    Scripture references on ushering as an opening devotional for the
    initial meeting: Psalm 81:1, 4, 10; 2 Kings 22:4; 1 Chronicles 9:19;

and Ezekiel 40:45−46. Also, brainstorm with a group of people all the problems you can think of with regard to ushering in your church. Make a list, and then make copies for use in the training session. Close the session with everyone reading "An Usher's Prayer" in unison.

TWO

The Functions of an Usher

The unpardonable sin of a church usher is inattention. Signals and communications are missed, people's needs are ignored, and the quality of an usher's effectiveness drops to zero when his mind wanders. Paul's admonition in Colossians 3:23–24 includes ushers: "Whatever you do, work at it with all your heart, as working for the Lord. . . . It is the Lord Christ you are serving."

THREE AREAS OF CONCENTRATION

No less concentration is needed by the usher than is necessary for the pastor, organist, pianist, choir director, soloist, or teacher. In this ministry there are three areas of concentration.

Concentrate on the People

Since most people tend to sit in the same place week after week, ushers should memorize regular attendees' usual places. Prompt, direct seating of people in their usual places is an indication of the usher's awareness. Seating visitors next to regular churchgoers with a word of introduction is helpful to new people. Awareness of empty seats in this general seating pattern comes only by concentration. If ushers were ranked like people in the military, a promotion should be given to every usher who learns to concentrate on people's names.

Concentrate on the Service

A church usher must be able to concentrate both on the people he is serving and on the church service in progress. Since every part of a worship service makes its own contribution to the total worship experience, the usher should know what is going on at any given moment and why it has been planned. Here are some common worship service elements:

❏ *Worship begins with reverent quietness.* During the last moments before the service begins, many congregations sit in quiet reverence, relaxing their minds and bodies while they meditate. In these precious moments of quietness, devout Christians have the opportunity to pray, think, and read their Bibles. Everything an usher does in these moments should help contribute to this atmosphere.

❏ *Call to worship.* A call to worship by the choir or an invocation by the pastor helps bring worshipers to attention and directs their thoughts to God. No person should be seated during the call to worship.

❏ *Congregational singing.* Beginning with the Protestant Reformation, singing has become an important means for praise and worship. Since the congregation often stands up to sing, this is one of the best times to seat latecomers.

❏ *Scripture reading.* Seating worshipers during the reading of the Bible is an indication of thoughtless irreverence. The usher may prevent people from being seated and may himself concentrate on the reading of Scripture by standing firmly at the head of the aisle during the Bible reading.

❏ *The pastoral prayer.* Nothing done in the morning service is more important than the pastor's prayer for the people. Representing every worshiper in the service, the pastor offers praises and petitions to God during some of the most sacred moments of the service. This is not the time for ushers to check the heat or run errands. It is to their spiritual advantage to participate in this prayer.

❏ *The ministry of music.* Anthems; praise band, orchestral, or choral arrangements; solos; and ensembles are used to carry out a special ministry in music. No one is seated during these moments because of the distraction to both the singers and listeners.

❏ *Offertory.* By the time the offering is received, most late-comers already have been seated. The offering is a means of worship and expresses the congregation's most tangible indication of commitment.

❏ *Moments of meditation.* After the pastor has read the sermon text or announced the theme of the message, worshipers are often asked to bow their heads in quiet thought. This not only serves to help prepare them for the sermon but also gives opportunity for them to hear the Holy Spirit's voice. Everyone, including ushers, should be still.

❏ *Sermon.* Although ushers' duties continue throughout the entire service, they should listen attentively to the message.

❏ *Invitation hymn.* An attitude of prayerful attention on the part of the ushers is an aid to the invitation. Also, they may assist persons to come forward for prayer. In some churches ushers have received instruction in one-on-one ministry.

❑ *Final benediction.* The last act of worship in most services is a prayer of divine blessing on the people as they leave the sanctuary. The final amen in this prayer is a cue to the ushers for all doors to be opened and preparations made for helping people exit the church.

The church usher who concentrates on what is happening in the service will do a more effective job and will receive more help from the service for himself. Ushering does not require ushers to be detached from or immune to the means of grace.

Concentrate on Yourself

Self-centered conceit is repulsive, but self-assurance and self-respect are admired. The usher who concentrates on the people and the church service will find it easy to concentrate on his own relationship to both. Here is a church usher's checklist:

Grooming

❑ Clean and refreshed
❑ Gum removed
❑ Hair groomed
❑ Clean shaven, or beard well trimmed
❑ Clothing clean and pressed (in the appropriate style for your church, whether that means a suit and tie or more casual clothes)
❑ Shoes shined

Assignment

- ❏ Arrive on time
- ❏ Never leave post
- ❏ Do not assume authority
- ❏ Concentrate on the service
- ❏ Pay special attention to guests
- ❏ Stock adequate supply of envelopes, hymnals, bulletins, and other materials
- ❏ Follow instructions

Attitude

- ❏ Proud to be an usher
- ❏ Optimistic about *our* church
- ❏ Pleasant conversationalist
- ❏ Pleasant face
- ❏ Nonjudgmental attitude
- ❏ Prayerful

AMBASSADOR OF KINDNESS

Since an usher's contacts are made directly with individuals, it's important that he learn to think with kindness and understanding about persons. He should not expect too much from them. An effective usher learns how to accept people as they are instead of the way he wishes they were. For instance, since it is the nature of some teenagers to be thoughtless, fickle, detached, bored, and even rebellious, the usher will not help these teenagers or the church's ministry by thinking unkind thoughts about them. Allowing teens and children to be true to their nature without censure or criticism may be more helpful than lecturing them on how they ought to behave.

Another special group in the church is the elderly. They often need more reassurance than young adults with growing families. Awareness of their special needs—especially their vision and hearing problems—is like a cup of cold water given in Jesus' name.

Perhaps the people who most need an usher's attention are first-time visitors. Many deplorable stories have been told about the encounters of new people with church ushers. It doesn't take much effort to say, "Hello." A smiling welcome— "We hope you'll enjoy the service today"—may be as reassuring to a visitor as a lifeline to a person in deep water. Identification of coatrooms and rest rooms, along with a word of introduction to one or two church members, may mean the difference between anxiety and a happy adjustment for the new visitor.

Kindness in conversation is something that ushers can develop. Negative statements that tend to be judgmental and smack of criticism are the very opposite of kindness. Here are some examples:

Negative: "You can't go in now!"
Positive: "We'll seat you in just a moment."

Negative: "You're late; you'll have to sit in the back!"
Positive: "Since the service has started, we have a place for you near the back."

Negative: "You can't stand here in everybody's way!"
Positive: "Would you like to visit over here where people won't interfere with your conversation?"

Negative: "At your age, I suppose you need a hearing aid!"
Positive: "We have some good seats up front where everyone can see and hear well."

Negative: "You teenagers, shut up!"
Positive: "Would you be willing to help us promote reverence in the sanctuary?"

A word of caution about expressing kindness: Ushers should be careful not to place their hands on people either in persuasion or familiarity. Let kindness come from the heart instead of the hands!

SEATING PEOPLE

An usher's main function is to seat people. The following six steps are intended to guide ushers in performing this function efficiently:

1. Ushers should arrive about thirty minutes before service time to receive their door and aisle assignments from the head usher. After surveying their section to be sure that the pew racks are stocked with envelopes, hymnals, Bibles, pencils, and other materials, the ushers take their supply of church bulletins and begin their seating responsibilities with the arrival of the first worshiper. Aisle assignments continue until the end of the service, even though ushers may be seated after the offering has been received.

2. The ushers should seat people as close to the front and center as seems appropriate. Back seats can always be filled with people coming in later, but it's often difficult to secure the cooperation of latecomers in being seated in the front. Never fill the sanctuary from the back to the front. Many churches use ropes to reserve the last three pews in the sanctuary for latecomers. However, if people insist on being seated near the back, it's better to have them in the rear than not to have them there at all.

3. When people arrive at the head of the aisle to be seated, an usher should give them a friendly recognition and then suggest a plan for seating them. For instance, he may say, "I'd like to seat you about halfway down." Or, "I have two seats on the aisle." Or, "I believe you'll enjoy the service more if you are seated near the front." People tend to respond with cooperation to a suggestion. But if the usher falls into the trap of asking people, "Where would you like to be seated?" he is in trouble. This may throw them into the same kind of dilemma people face in trying to choose from a menu.

4. The usher should walk slowly down the aisle, stopping at the pew where the people are to be seated and forming a little gate into the seating area by placing his hand on the back of the pew in front. If the usher walks too fast, people will lag behind and feel very much alone. They may even slip into a seat nearer the back and leave the usher standing in the aisle with no one to seat. There is dignity in walking slowly, and it's a good idea for people to be close enough to whisper a question or word of instruction to the usher if need be. In all cases, the usher does not give a church bulletin to the worshiper until

after he or she is seated. This keeps the usher in charge, even if people desert the usher to find a seat on their own.

5. There are two basic rules in seating the congregation: (1) The usher never allows any diversion to keep him from being aware of the people who arrive at the head of his aisle for seating. He never leaves his station or lapses into inattention. (2) An usher never points to a seat and sends people down the aisle by themselves. He shows them to their seats personally.

6. There are several ways to be sure an usher is on hand at the head of the aisle at all times for seating people. In large churches with long aisles, two ushers sometimes stand at the head of the aisle to greet people and then direct them to another usher who is halfway down the aisle ready to seat them. In other churches a roving usher is stationed halfway between two aisles and steps to the assistance of his colleagues whenever needed. This roving usher in reality works in two aisles of the church. In small churches, one usher per aisle is all that is needed.

THE CHURCH OFFERING

At least since the days of Paul, taking a collection in church has been a regular part of worship: "Now about the collection for God's people: . . . On the first day of every week, each one of you should set aside a sum of money in keeping with his income" (1 Corinthians 16:1–2). The church offering consists of the following five factors:

1. *Processional.* In most churches the ushers who seat the people receive the offering in their same aisle. Some churches,

however, use a separate set of ushers who are seated on the very front pew, ready for their assignment when the offering time comes. Ordinarily the pastor will make some introductory remarks or read a Scripture passage to prepare the minds of the people for giving. (See appendix 2 for a listing of thirty Scripture passages that can be used as part of the introductory remarks.) Then, on a signal given by the head usher or the pastor, the processional of ushers begins. With a little practice, the ushers can walk in step and keep abreast as they proceed from the rear of the sanctuary to the front. Precision in this procedure is the mark of discipline among ushers.

2. *Distribution of the offering plates.* In some churches the head usher distributes offering plates to the ushers in the rear of the sanctuary, and they carry the plates under their right arms as they proceed to the front. In other churches the offering plates are on the Communion table as symbols of worship and are distributed by the pastor or lay officer.

3. *Blessing or dedication.* If ushers carry offering plates with them to the front of the sanctuary, they usually stop in line with the first pew. If a prayer of blessing and thanksgiving is prayed before the offering is received, the ushers stand reverently in their places until the pastor has concluded the prayer. (See appendix 2 for several sample prayers you can use to help form your own offertory prayers.) If the offering plates are distributed from the Communion table, the ushers must proceed to the front and center of the sanctuary to receive their plates and wait reverently for the prayer of blessing. As a third alternative, in some churches the ushers carry their offering plates with them from the rear of the sanctuary and proceed immediately

to receive the offering, beginning with the first pew and working toward the rear.

After the offering is received, the plates are given to two ushers, who bring them down the center aisle to stand before the Communion table where a prayer of dedication is offered by the pastor. The offering then is placed on the Communion table until the service is over. The return of the ushers to the front of the sanctuary is often accompanied by the congregation's standing to sing the doxology. If the pastor prefers to pray for the offering before it is received, the offering plates are turned over to the head usher or other church officials who are responsible to count and deposit the funds. Informal, haphazard ushering during the offering is an indication of an unplanned service and a failure to perceive giving as a means of grace.

4. *Receiving of the collection.* Here again there is room for variety of procedure. Ordinarily there is one usher to an aisle who works pews on both sides of the aisle at the same time. Only in churches with special seating problems should the offering plates be handed back by the worshipers from one pew to another. If on occasion an offering plate is dropped by a worshiper, it is typically the job of the head usher to retrieve the funds and handle the situation while the regular ushers continue their collection assignment.

5. *Offertory.* Regardless of the procedures used in the processional, the prayer, distribution of the plates, and the actual collection, the offertory is a means of grace and should be played out to its conclusion. Background music is for elevators and dining rooms, but an offertory is a ministry of music.

MISCELLANEOUS FUNCTIONS

Besides the ushers' major duties in seating people and receiving the collection, there are many other smaller functions of vital importance. Here are a few:

Hearing Devices

The ushers have authority and responsibility in the distribution and use of hearing devices among those who need them. This means knowledge of equipment, ensuring ample space for storage, and commitment to alertness in making the equipment available.

Children Who Leave the Service

Children should learn very early that it is not permissible to wander in and out of the sanctuary. Children who come from an unchurched background and are seated apart from supervising adults often especially need instruction. Ushers must treat these children very kindly, but children cannot be allowed to disturb the service. Either provide seating for wandering children in the back of the sanctuary or provide them with special chairs in the foyer so they will not disturb other worshipers by returning to their seats.

When one child leaves the service, a procession of others usually follows. Tact and understanding are necessary in handling this rather delicate problem, but children can be taught to stay in the sanctuary throughout the entire service. People who have special physical problems that make it necessary for them occasionally to leave the service should be seated near the rear.

Seating of Latecomers

Latecomers should be seated during the singing of the hymns but never during the reading of Scripture or during the ministry of music. Latecomers who arrive after the sermon has begun should be seated as inconspicuously as possible. Reserved seats in the back can be a big help in alleviating this problem in many churches.

Registering of Guests

In many churches the ushers are wholly or partially responsible for the registering of guests. Although the system and techniques must be worked out in detail with the pastor and head usher, procedures must include means for identifying guests on sight, making registration materials available to the guests, and turning the results over to the pastor or church office. Many churches use cards while others use guest books. Some use both. The important thing is to make a guest feel welcome. Some guests do not want to be identified, and in this case their privacy should be respected.

Checking of Rest Rooms

Checks should be made on all rest rooms before and after services to see that they are clean and well supplied with toilet paper and hand towels. Since many churches operate with a minimal number of rest room facilities, deterioration can show up very quickly.

Handling of "Characters"

Alcoholics, vagrants, and other types of characters sometimes drift into churches, expecting to reap the benefits of

Christian humanitarianism. These situations must be handled kindly but firmly without involving the pastor. Most city churches, which have a greater share of this kind of problem, have detailed procedures already outlined.

Emergency Procedures

Procedures for dealing with physical sickness, fire, power failure, and other emergencies should be planned in advance. Telephone numbers for the police department, fire department, public utilities, and ambulance services should be readily available. Fire extinguishers, flashlights, candles, and matches should be on hand. And even more important are the procedures worked out in advance by the ushers.

Parking Problems

In some churches ushers are responsible for helping people with any parking problems. Identifying apparel, such as fluorescent vests or slickers, should be worn by ushers who park cars for people or who direct drivers to available parking spots. In some instances the same people double as traffic control officers when parking lots adjoin busy streets or highways.

Communion Services

In some churches ushers participate in the distribution of the elements in Communion services. In general the same techniques are used as in receiving the offering. In serving the Lord's Supper, however, twice as many people are needed because of the distribution of both the bread and the wine. Details for this service should be worked out carefully and completely between the pastor and head usher. Many churches make charts of their seating arrangements and assign people to specific responsibilities. The goal in this distribution is to serve everyone as quickly as possible but in an atmosphere of devotional dignity.

Record Keeping

Keeping accurate attendance records is considered the ushers' responsibility in most churches. Record forms are included among the ushers' supplies. An accurate record of attendance must be broken down to include all areas of the church where people can be found. Besides the seating sections of the sanctuary, this record form should include the platform, choir, children's churches, nurseries, ushers on duty, and a miscellaneous item to cover persons in the hallways or on special assignment outside the sanctuary. The form also may include a place for a special note about weather or other conditions and circumstances affecting attendance. It is important to take this count in as inconspicuous a manner as possible. Some people resent being counted, and the process can become a distraction to the service.

Funerals

Pallbearers ordinarily do not serve as ushers. Funerals held in mortuary chapels are usually ushered by the staff on duty, but in a church funeral, the church's ushers often are needed to help seat the mourners. Church funerals are often larger than those held in mortuary chapels. In fact, ushers may have the challenge of seating an overflow congregation. Quiet, efficient ushers will be needed under the general supervision of the funeral director. The funeral director will alert the ushers to any special seating arrangements desired by the family.

Overflow Congregations

Special occasions such as Easter, Christmas, union services, and special denominational meetings often result in an attendance that overflows the main sanctuary. Dignity and preparedness on the part of the ushers will help expedite any problems that might arise. If the plan for extra seats involves folding chairs, they should be readily available and placed in use by a prearranged plan. If balconies, foyers, and extra rooms are used for these occasions, the head usher should determine when each move is made to fill additional space. Lighting, heating and cooling, use of hymnals, amplified sound, and other needs should be thought through in advance. Informal conferences among ushers and disorganized "scurrying about" tend to be a distraction.

QUESTIONS FOR REFLECTION AND DISCUSSION

1. Read Matthew 14:13−23 alone or together as a group of ushers. What kind of ushering did Jesus need for the feeding of the five thousand?

2. How can studying the bulletin to gain a better understanding of the order of your morning and evening worship services help your ushers do their work more effectively?

3. Are there some things that could be done to increase reverence in the sanctuary and smoothness of operation in the mechanics of the church service? Share with your pastor any ideas you come up with.

4. Ask your pastor to explain to your ushers the deeper meaning of the elements of worship indicated on pages 26−28.

5. What is the worst ushering situation you've ever experienced?

6. How would your ushers respond to the following problems? Role-play two different responses, one in which an usher is patient and speaks kindly and the other in which he is abrupt and speaks unkindly.
    *   Latecomer

    *   Offering plate dropped

    *   Slow moving

    *   Loud talking

    *   Crying baby

    *   Child leaving service

THREE

An Usher's Standard of Excellence

THE PERSONALITY OF A CHURCH

Churches have different personalities, just like people do. The three determinants of human personality are (1) biological factors, (2) environmental factors, and (3) the inner self. This soul, or inner self, consists of attitudes, emotions, and will. The self interacts with the biological and environmental factors, making changes where possible and constantly adjusting to the experiences of life.

In a similar way the character and personality of a church depends on (1) physical factors, (2) environmental factors, and (3) the inner self. The physical factors include the church building, with its capacities, its limitations, and its structural strengths and weaknesses. The environmental factors include the location of the church and its general setting in the community. In a church the inner self consists of its ministries— preaching, teaching, music, and ushering—and the combined attitudes, feelings, and wills of the people. In a church, the mind of Christ—under the guidance of the Holy Spirit—functions through people as they interact with each other, their environment, and the physical church building where they worship and work. The will of the people plus their attitudes and feelings determine the standard of excellence at all levels in the church. Thus, everything pertaining to the church, including the janitorial service, sound management, worship leading, multimedia presentations, bulletin content and design, business procedures, congregational singing, special singing, preaching, teaching, facilities and equipment, and all else is a reflection of the church's standard of excellence. This standard of excellence is obvious in the ministry of ushering.

A MORE EXCELLENT WAY

After discussing the spiritual gifts at length, Paul said, "And now I will show you the most excellent way" (1 Corinthians 12:31). Paul then explained the importance of Christian love and listed some characteristics of love that also happen to apply to the ministry of ushering.

1. *"Love is patient."* Personnel problems can become irksome, even among church ushers. Inefficiency, bothersome habits, or tendencies of other ushers to assume responsibility beyond their authority may create negative feelings within the board of ushers. Paul's only antidote for this is to accept people as they are instead of wishing they were different.

2. *"Love is kind."* Part of an usher's role is to absorb criticisms people may not have had a chance to verbalize to other church officials. Some people, even churchgoers, are difficult to get along with. The test of excellence among church ushers is not their capacity to separate the good from the bad but to continue being kind when others are difficult.

3. *"Love does not boast."* An usher who makes a display of his own worth through boasting and bragging is concentrating more on the impression he is making than on the people he is serving.

4. *"Love is not proud. . . . It is not self-seeking."* A conceited, self-centered usher is below the standard of excellence for a Spirit-filled church.

5. *"Love is not rude."* Regardless of the emergency, a good usher never loses his head. Stability and poise are characteristics of a high standard.

6. *"Love is not easily angered."* Enough annoying things happen in any church to provoke the negative emotions of an usher, but an usher with a high standard of excellence maintains an attitude of positive regard.

7. *"Love does not delight in evil but rejoices with the truth."* Every church usher is either a part of the problem or a part of the solution. He is either more critical than helpful or more helpful than critical. Stopping rumors, rejoicing in good reports, and always maintaining Christian optimism are characteristic of his standard of excellence.

8. *"Love always protects, always trusts, always hopes, always perseveres."* One of the differences between a good usher and a poor one is the capacity to deal effectively with problems. If there were no problems, there would be no need for ushers, yet some ushers become critical, irritated, and upset at the first irregularity in their assignment. Being able to handle frustration, to make decisions quickly, and to work under pressure are desirable qualities in an usher.

9. *"Love never fails."* One quality that helps eliminate stress in any kind of ushering emergency is human understanding. Value judgments, verbal explanations, excuses, and all other weapons used for handling emergencies can't compare to an understanding heart.

10. *"And now these three remain: faith, hope and love. But the greatest of these is love."* An abiding faith, an optimistic outlook, and a love for God and people are all important in the standard of excellence set down by Paul. But of these three great qualities, the usher's highest good is his love of God, which is reflected in the usher's capacity to love people just as they are.

EXHIBITING THE FRUIT OF THE SPIRIT

"The fruit of the Spirit is love, joy, peace, patience, kindness, goodness, faithfulness, gentleness and self-control. Against such things there is no law" (Galatians 5:22–23). A church usher who becomes a useful representative of Jesus Christ in the sanctuary will desire to possess qualities that do not come by law but by the indwelling presence of the Holy Spirit.

1. *"The fruit of the Spirit is love."* The New Testament love Paul was writing about was a spirit of consideration and respect that did not depend on the attitudes or behavior of the other person. As one person put it, "The Holy Spirit can even help you love the person you do not like." This kind of love is not dependent on the other person's actions or reactions but only on the attitudes of the one who loves. Ushers should never be involved in church strife.

2. *"The fruit of the Spirit is joy."* Cold, aloof, mechanical ushering is depressing to churchgoers. But the sight of an effective usher who radiates joy is a heartwarming experience for any worshiper.

3. *"The fruit of the Spirit is peace."* The presence of a good church usher adds to the peace and calm of every situation. His

presence is reassuring, and his efficient way of dealing with situations tends to minimize problems.

4. *"The fruit of the Spirit is patience."* Patience is one of the great qualities of a good usher. The church building itself, the environment around the church, the ministry of the church, and the people in the congregation may all provide challenges to an usher's patience, but the long-suffering usher chooses to remain hopeful and persevering in all kinds of situations.

5. *"The fruit of the Spirit is kindness."* No good usher ever throws around his authority. Instead, he takes on the role of a servant and seeks to meet kindly the needs of all people—from noisy children to cranky senior citizens. While he concentrates on the needs of others, he forgets about himself and humbly goes about his assignment.

6. *"The fruit of the Spirit is goodness."* The Lord doesn't exhort people to be intelligent, clever, or rich. But he does in many places in his Word indicate that a basic quality of the Spirit-filled person is human goodness. Deception in any of its forms is incompatible with Christian goodness.

7. *"The fruit of the Spirit is faithfulness."* Faithfulness is essential to excellence in ushering. Being on time, taking initiative, planning ahead, and communicating with those who are in authority are qualities of people who take their ministry of ushering seriously.

8. *"The fruit of the Spirit is gentleness."* Hallmarks of a Christian gentleman include thoughtfulness, discretion, pleasant language, and constant courtesy.

9. *"The fruit of the Spirit is self-control."* Self-control among excellent ushers is manifested in a variety of ways, from

cleanliness and good grooming to one's speech and general demeanor.

10. *"Against such things there is no law."* No head usher or pastor can write enough rules to cover every situation ushers may face. However, ushers who are filled with God's Spirit will naturally bear fruit that will guide them in knowing what to do and say in a variety of situations.

SACRED MOMENTS

Prayer, Scripture reading, and the ministry of music are among the sacred moments in every church service. By the ushers' example of quiet attention, they can help make these moments more meaningful to everyone. Movement in the building should be stopped as much as possible while all thoughts and actions are centered on talking with God, hearing from God through his Word, and receiving the ministry of music.

EQUIPMENT AND SUPPLIES

To be effective in their ministry, ushers need certain equipment and supplies. The following list will serve as a starter.

❏ *Ushers' desk and storage facility.* Much like the bell captain in a hotel lobby, the head usher of a church needs a center of operation. It should be located in a convenient spot where people may come when they have questions and need information. It may contain the guest register, but it must contain storage space for all kinds of supplies used regularly by the ushers, as well as room for emergency equipment. This is the place for the intercom that connects the pastor with the ushers; it could possibly contain a telephone available for use by church members as necessary.

❏ *Envelopes, guest cards, and writing materials.* Each usher may be responsible for filling the racks on the backs of the pews of his section. Also, there are many times when writing materials, even for congregational distribution, are needed. These should be purchased in quantity and kept in storage by the head usher. Church offering envelopes, blank checks, and pens or pencils are also needed among this equipment.

❏ *Identifying badges.* In some churches ushers wear an identifying flower in their suit lapels. Others prefer an identifying badge or name tag. But in all instances ushers should be equipped with some identifying badge or symbol.

❏ *First-aid equipment.* Congregations that have a large number of children are especially likely to have to deal with accidents. Equipment for handling emergencies should be in the possession of the head usher and stored at the ushers' desk.

❏ *Lost and found.* The ushers' central facility should have room for lost and found items.

QUESTIONS FOR REFLECTION AND DISCUSSION

1. Read Mark 10:13–16 alone or together as a group of ushers. How important is it to be kind to children? What can you do to increasingly show kindness to the children in your church?

2. What is your church's personality? As you reflect on and discuss this, be sure to include the issues of physical property, community and regional environment, and the general attitudes of the congregation about your church.

3. How can your ushers capitalize even more on the "sacred moments" (see page 48) in your church services?

FOUR

The Authority and Responsibility of Ushers

Authority and *responsibility* are two factors that cannot be separated in the carrying out of a duty, at least not without losing a high degree of effectiveness. If a person is given responsibility for a specific job but never the authority to implement it, the result is usually utter frustration. And if a person is the designated authority for a specific job but is never given the responsibility, disorganization is most often the result. For ushers to do a good job in any local church, the areas of their responsibility and authority should be clearly understood. Ushers who assume authority beyond their responsibility create confusion, while ushers who do not accept the authority to fulfill their responsibility are ineffective. Therefore, the following areas of authority and responsibility should be understood fully by the pastor, church board, head usher, ushers, and even the congregation.

THE ULTIMATE AUTHORITY

In most churches the final authority for the operation of the church centers in the pastor and church board. Because pastors and church boards cannot do everything that needs to be done, they delegate considerable authority and responsibility to laypeople. Ushers are one group of people to whom authority and responsibility are delegated, and the pastor or church board usually appoints a head usher who is given responsibility and authority over ushering.

THE HEAD USHER

The head usher needs to be a person of considerable maturity and Christian character. He should feel comfortable with the pastor and the church, and since he may oversee the work of many people, he must have the ability to work well with others. Furthermore, he should be well accepted among the general population of the church. Once this man is chosen, he should be given full authority and responsibility for the ushering job, referring back to the church board and pastor only on matters of policy.

Recruitment

The head usher should have authority to recruit his own ushers, for he will work best with people he has chosen. Even if there are already certain persons on the board of ushers whom he would not like to keep, the authority to make his own decisions leaves him the full responsibility for his actions. He should not feel that specific ushers were handed to him without his consultation and acceptance. After studying the total situation, he may decide to keep all the ushers from a previous year, but the decision should be his. Also, the head usher may want to choose more than one board of ushers. Some churches use a separate set of ushers for Sunday school, morning worship, and evening worship. Still others rotate their ushers on a three-month assignment basis. The head usher must not only decide on the people he will use but also on the system for assigning their responsibilities.

General Supervision

Once people have been recruited to serve as church ushers, it is the responsibility of the head usher to supervise all their functions. The head usher becomes the channel through whom the pastor works. Ushers with special problems do not take them directly to the pastor or the board but to the head usher. But unless the channels of communication are made crystal clear, the authority and responsibility of the head usher in this regard will be thwarted. The pastor and others should not be giving instructions directly to ushers but always through the head usher.

Church Government: Authority and Responsibility

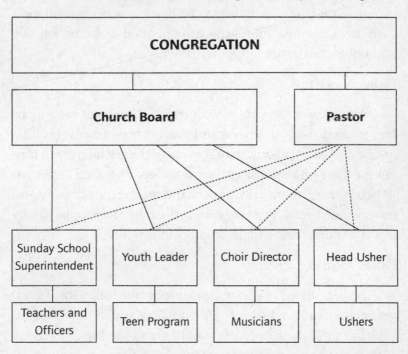

While working in consultation with the pastor, lay leaders must have both responsibility and authority for their assignments.

Assignments

After learning more about his ushers, the head usher will make specific assignments to each one. These may be annual assignments or rotating assignments on the basis of the head usher's judgment. Any usher who cannot fulfill his assignment on a given day should make phone contact with the head usher as early as possible so that a substitute may be recruited. In consultation with the pastor and the ushers, the head usher can determine how early ushers should arrive to begin their assignments. Rules governing the conduct and methods of the ushers should be worked out by the head usher in consultation with them, because rules arbitrarily handed down by a heavy hand of authority are often ineffective.

Usher Meetings

Many head ushers meet with their ushers once each quarter for discussion on general and specific assignments. At least once each year it is good to make one of these gatherings a dinner meeting with spouses present. Ushers may do a better job if their spouses more fully understand their responsibility. And ushers always work together better when they have opportunity to share a meal and discuss matters informally.

Other Duties

The head usher is also responsible for the following: supervising the information center and lost and found station, counting attendees, ordering supplies, and serving as a liaison with the pastor during the service.

INDIVIDUAL USHERS

Each usher has a right to know exactly what is required of him. He needs to know when he is to arrive, what his aisle assignment is, and how long he is to stay at his post. He must be trained in the techniques the head usher chooses to use in seating the people and receiving the offering. If an usher reaches beyond his responsibility and authority, problems arise. Adjusting the heat, opening windows, closing doors, bringing in additional chairs, operating in another usher's aisle of responsibility, and passing on unnecessary opinions are some of the ways ushers can create problems. But an usher who assumes the authority and fulfills the responsibility given him in a specific assignment is a man of God who is rendering a meaningful Christian service.

KNOW YOUR CHURCH

Since ushers deal directly with individual churchgoers, it is crucial for them to know many things about their church that may not be known by other laypersons. Ushers will be asked many questions for which they'll be able to provide answers if they are familiar with information on the following topics:

- ❏ Church office hours
- ❏ Lost and found locations
- ❏ Bus schedules
- ❏ Parking
- ❏ Rest room locations
- ❏ Classroom locations

❏ Church nursery location and policies for use

❏ Location of a phone

❏ Location of first-aid supplies

❏ Pastor's educational and professional background

❏ The church manual or book of discipline

❏ Church denominational headquarters

In an ushers' meeting, you may want to use a blackboard or large pad of paper to list the kinds of information ushers are asked for most often with regard to the church.

In all churches, but especially in large ones, it's good for ushers to know their local church building in great detail, including all the locations listed above, as well as the locations of heating, plumbing, and electrical controls.

QUESTIONS FOR REFLECTION AND DISCUSSION

1. How clearly do you think your ushers understand the areas of their responsibility and authority? What can you do to provide a greater understanding if there seems to be a need in this area?

2. Does your church have a head usher? Is this area of authority understood by your church ministry staff and board, as well as by the usher teams? What are some things you can do to reorganize your usher teams in order to do ministry more effectively?

3. Do your ushers know what is required of them? What are some ways you might be able to communicate clearly the expectations regarding ushers' responsibilities?

4. How well do your ushers know your church? Review the list on pages 55–56. Perhaps you'll want to put together a document that contains the answers to some of the topics on the list, as well as a diagram of your church that shows locations for classes, materials, supplies, and heating and lighting controls.

FIVE

Ushers as Greeters

Even in churches that have greeters who are not part of the ushering team, greeting is still at least a partial responsibility of every usher. Ushers who can greet regular attendees by name and can remember the names of visitors long enough to introduce them to others have reached a high standard of excellence. Here are some things for ushers to consider when greeting people.

REMEMBERING NAMES

Most people profess to have difficulty in remembering names. Many ushers say, "I just can't remember people's names, only their faces." Probably the best way to put names with faces is to study a pictorial church directory if one is available. The ushers' desk should have copies of the church directory containing a list of members' names, addresses, and phone numbers. Four more tips are given here to aid ushers in remembering names:

1. *Create enough interest in a person to listen to his name until it is accurately understood in your own mind.* Most people do not know the names of other persons because they do not truly listen. If necessary, ask the individual to repeat his or her name and perhaps even to spell it.

2. *Relate the name to someone or something that has special meaning.* The person's name may be the same as that of a special friend or relative. Or a name may be a reminder of a place or an experience. Although many jokes have been told about

confusion that may result from relating names to people, places, and things, it still is an excellent mnemonic tool.

3. *Use the person's name at least three times as soon as possible.* Call the person by name as you speak to her. Use the person's name while introducing her to someone else. Tell someone else about the person you've met, using her name as you tell of the experience of meeting her.

4. *Write down the name.* One traveling preacher who was noted for remembering thousands of names used several mnemonic techniques. One of the most important things he did was to write down the name in his notebook as soon as he was alone. After using a person's name several times and then writing it in his notebook, he found it much easier to remember. And in case of a memory lapse, he always had a ready reference.

CONCENTRATING ON THE OTHER PERSON

Although your time may be limited, concentrate fully on the visitor you are greeting. Look the visitor in the eye, smile, shake hands warmly, and above all let your conversation focus on him. Do not let everything he says remind you of something about yourself. Talk optimistically and happily about your church. Think of good things you can say enthusiastically about your pastor and the people in your church, and let these things become a part of your conversation with all visitors.

INTRODUCING PEOPLE TO ONE ANOTHER

After greeting new people, make every effort not to leave them standing alone at the end of your conversation. If possible, leave them in a conversation with someone to whom you have introduced them. The more people a new person can meet in the church, the more possibilities there are for building bridges of understanding and fellowship that may cause the visitor to want to return. As far as possible, try to introduce visitors to people who may have some mutual interests. Young couples like to meet other young couples. Single young people like to meet other single young people. People in business or in a particular profession enjoy meeting other people in similar businesses or professions.

Introducing persons need not be a threatening situation. There are just a few traditional rules of etiquette to remember (though your particular church culture may lend itself to a more informal approach of introducing people):

1. *Begin an introduction by calling the name of the honored person.* For instance: "Dr. Famous, I want you to meet Mr. Lesser-Known." Your pastor, visiting church dignitaries, older citizens, and well-known persons are among those who are honored, and therefore their name is typically mentioned first in an introduction.

2. *Introduce people of lower seniority, younger age, or lesser distinction to people of higher seniority, greater age, or greater distinction.* For instance: "Mrs. Old-Timer, I'd like you to meet Mrs. Newcomer"; "Mr. Older, I want to introduce you to Ms. Younger"; "Reverend Doctor, this is Mr. Custodian."

3. *Use full names.* It is generally not good etiquette to use either first names or last names by themselves in introductions. Informal warmth surely is a social grace in any church, but a lack of respect is not. Informal use of first names develops as

friendship grows, but the use of a person's last name without his first name and title is never a sign of respect.

VERY IMPORTANT PERSONS

On occasion there are visitors in the congregation whose presence should be made known to the pastor. Some discreet communication system can be devised for keeping the pastor informed. A note from the ushers to the pastor at the time the collection is received is one of the most common means for this type of communication. Obviously, the pastor will use his own discretion in the public recognition of visitors.

QUESTIONS FOR REFLECTION AND DISCUSSION

1. How well do your ushers remember names? If they need some help, try this: show the ushers a series of pictures (from magazine advertisements) of men, women, and families. Explain a little about each one and introduce these people by name. Test your ushers later by showing the pictures again to see how many names they can remember. With practice their ability to remember should increase.

2. How well do your ushers introduce people to each other? Role-play with your ushers different ways of introducing people, based on the suggestions found on page 61.

APPENDIX 1

An Usher's Checklist

BEFORE THE SERVICE

Setting Up in the Sanctuary

____ Open the doors and turn on the lights (if the custodian hasn't already done so).

____ Put up the hymn numbers on the display boards where necessary.

____ Bring the offering plates to their designated spots.

____ Make sure the hearing aids and large-print Bibles and hymnals are in their designated spots for pick-up by those who desire to use them.

____ Gather the weekly bulletins and make sure you have the correct ones.

____ Review the order of worship so that you'll be prepared for all activities.

____ Deliver bulletins to various choirs that may be participating and to other areas of the church as needed, such as nurseries and children's worship centers.

Greeting and Seating Worshipers

____ Make sure your name tag is on.

____ Station yourself at your assigned door.

____ Greet people as they arrive.

_____ Be prepared to direct people to the information center, nursery, children's worship centers, rest rooms, and classrooms as necessary.

_____ Escort people to their seats, making sure they have a bulletin (and the children have a children's bulletin, if available).

DURING THE SERVICE

_____ Avoid seating people during an opening processional or call to worship or during opening prayers.

_____ At the designated time, pick up the offering plates and receive the offering (if your church uses ushers for the offering).

_____ Count the number of people in attendance at the service (if your church keeps a record of attendance).

_____ Assist in the movement of worshipers from their seats to the Communion table, and back again (if your church invites people to come forward and uses ushers to assist).

_____ Attend to any ongoing distractions or emergencies.

_____ Be prepared to adjust heating/cooling and lighting if needed.

_____ Check various areas in the church at points during the service (rest rooms, foyers, parking lots, and the like).

AFTER THE SERVICE

_____ Deliver the offering plates to the appropriate person or persons.

_____ Pick up all bulletins, paper, and pencils in the seats throughout the church and return Bibles and hymnals to the racks as necessary.

_____ Check and replace information cards in the racks as necessary.

_____ Collect attendance/prayer request folders and put in designated place for collating.

_____ Store in their designated spots the hearing aids and large-print Bibles and hymnals.

_____ Remove the hymn numbers from the display boards.

_____ Turn off the lights and close all sanctuary doors.

APPENDIX 2

Resources for the Offering

APPROPRIATE SCRIPTURES

The Scriptures offer rich resources to equip us to highlight the offering as an important part of the worship service. Here are thirty Scripture passages that can be used to introduce the offering or that can inform offertory prayers. These Scriptures may be introduced with a sentence or two of explanation, or with an illustration, followed by an offertory prayer.

Acts 20:35b — ". . . remembering the words the Lord Jesus himself said: 'It is more blessed to give than to receive.'"

Matthew 2:11 — "They saw the child with his mother Mary, and they bowed down and worshiped him. Then they opened their treasures and presented him with gifts of gold and of incense and of myrrh."

Matthew 6:19–21 — "Do not store up for yourselves treasures on earth, where moth and rust destroy, and where thieves break in and steal. But store up for yourselves treasures in heaven, where moth and rust do not destroy, and where thieves do not break in and steal. For where your treasure is, there your heart will be also."

1 Peter 4:10 — "Each one should use whatever gift he has received to serve others, faithfully administering God's grace in its various forms."

Acts 10:4 — "Your prayers and gifts to the poor have come up as a memorial offering before God."

Psalm 23:6 — "Surely goodness and love will follow me all the days of my life, and I will dwell in the house of the LORD forever."

Psalm 31:21 — "Praise be to the LORD, for he showed his wonderful love to me when I was in a besieged city."

Proverbs 3:9 — "Honor the LORD with your wealth, with the firstfruits of all your crops."

Proverbs 11:25 — "A generous man will prosper; he who refreshes others will himself be refreshed."

2 Corinthians 9:6 — "Remember this: Whoever sows sparingly will also reap sparingly, and whoever sows generously will also reap generously."

Deuteronomy 16:17 — "Each of you must bring a gift in proportion to the way the LORD your God has blessed you."

1 Corinthians 16:1–2 — "Now about the collection for God's people: Do what I told the Galatian churches to do. On the first day of every week, each one of you should set aside a sum of money in keeping with his income."

Malachi 3:8 — "Will a man rob God? Yet you rob me. But you ask, 'How do we rob you?' In tithes and offerings."

Malachi 3:10 — "Bring the whole tithe into the storehouse, that there may be food in my house. Test me in this, says the LORD Almighty, and see if I will not throw open the floodgates of heaven and pour out so much blessing that you will not have room enough for it."

Psalm 96:8 — "Ascribe to the LORD the glory due his name; bring an offering and come into his courts."

Psalm 116:12 — "How can I repay the LORD for all his goodness to me?"

Luke 12:48 — "From everyone who has been given much, much will be demanded; and from the one who has been entrusted with much, much more will be asked."

Luke 6:38 — "Give, and it will be given to you. A good measure, pressed down, shaken together and running over, will be poured into your lap. For with the measure you use, it will be measured to you."

Galatians 6:9 — "Let us not become weary in doing good, for at the proper time we will reap a harvest if we do not give up."

Genesis 14:18–20 — "Then Melchizedek king of Salem . . . blessed Abram, saying, 'Blessed be Abram by God Most High, Creator of heaven and earth. And blessed be God Most High, who delivered your enemies into your hand.' Then Abram gave him a tenth of everything."

Genesis 28:22 — "This stone that I have set up as a pillar will be God's house, and of all that you give me I will give you a tenth."

Mark 12:41 — "Jesus sat down opposite the place where the offerings were put and watched the crowd putting their money into the temple treasury. Many rich people threw in large amounts."

Mark 12:42–44—"But a poor widow came and put in two very small copper coins, worth only a fraction of a penny. Calling his disciples to him, Jesus said, 'I tell you the truth, this poor widow has put more into the treasury than all the others. They all gave out of their wealth; but she, out of her poverty, put in everything—all she had to live on.'"

Matthew 6:19–20—"Do not store up for yourselves treasures on earth, where moth and rust destroy, and where thieves break in and steal. But store up for yourselves treasures in heaven, where moth and rust do not destroy, and where thieves do not break in and steal."

Leviticus 27:30—"A tithe of everything from the land, whether grain from the soil or fruit from the trees, belongs to the LORD; it is holy to the LORD."

2 Corinthians 8:12—"For if the willingness is there, the gift is acceptable according to what one has, not according to what he does not have."

2 Corinthians 9:7—"Each man should give what he has decided in his heart to give, not reluctantly or under compulsion, for God loves a cheerful giver."

Hebrews 13:16—"Do not forget to do good and to share with others, for with such sacrifices God is pleased."

2 Samuel 24:24—"I will not sacrifice to the LORD my God burnt offerings that cost me nothing."

Psalm 116:12, 17–18—"How can I repay the Lord for all his goodness to me? . . . I will sacrifice a thank offering to you and call on the name of the Lord. I will fulfill my vows to the Lord in the presence of all his people."

APPROPRIATE OFFERTORY PRAYERS

Almighty God, the source of every good and perfect gift, accept the offerings which your people now present to you with willing and thankful hearts. Grant us the grace to set ourselves apart to your service, that we may glorify you this week and on into your heavenly kingdom. Through Jesus Christ our Lord. Amen.

———————

Father of mercies, who gave your beloved Son for the life of your people, and has given us all things richly to enjoy, help us as we present our offerings to do so with thankfulness, and to present ourselves for your service. Through Jesus Christ our Lord. Amen.

———————

Creator God, we know that you have made everything in this world. You have been and you are so generous to us each day. We pray that we here, your willing servants, your grateful creatures, will show our generosity in giving back to you that which is already yours. In Jesus' name. Amen.

———————

Lord God, from whom we receive both our gifts and the power to give, grant that these offerings which we now bring to you may be used for your glory and the building of your kingdom, through Jesus Christ our Lord. Amen.

———————

Grant us, Lord, hearts that give with gladness. Even as you gave your all for us, may we give our all to you. May our giving be a blessing and not a burden, so that we would be eager and willing givers of the gifts you have poured out on us. In Christ. Amen.

All that we have is from you, heavenly Father, for you are the creator and preserver of all people and things. Accept these gifts we now bring in your presence. Help us to make our whole lives an offering before you. We desire to seal this our worship in a renewed dedication of ourselves and our gifts and our time to your service. This we pray through Jesus Christ our Lord. Amen.

Touch our hearts, precious Father, with your love, so that we may sincerely desire to carry out the privilege of sharing our resources with others. May the grace you have shown us in Jesus Christ cause us to overflow with generosity in our giving. In Jesus' name. Amen.

We want to hear from you. Please send your comments about this book to us in care of the address below. Thank you.

ZONDERVAN™

GRAND RAPIDS, MICHIGAN 49530 USA

WWW.ZONDERVAN.COM